DECORATING WITH SILK & DRIED FLOWERS

80 Arrangements Using Floral Materials of All Kinds

The Home Decorating Institute®

COWLES
Creative Publishing, Inc.

Copyright © 1993 Cowles Creative Publishing, Inc., formerly Cy DeCosse Inc.
5900 Green Oak Drive Minnetonka, Minnesota 55343 • 1-800-328-3895 • All rights reserved • Printed in U.S.A.

Library of Congress Cataloging-in-Publication Data Decorating with silk & dried flowers. p. cm. — (Arts & crafts for home decorating) Includes index. ISBN 0-86573-361-9 ISBN 0-86573-362-7 (pbk.) 1. Dried flower arrangement. 2. Silk flowers. 3. Artificial flowers. 4. Flower arrangement. I. Cy DeCosse Incorporated. II. Title: Decorating with silk and dried flowers. III. Series. IV. Series: The home decorating institute. SB449.3.D7D43 1993 745.92 — dc20   93-25892

CONTENTS

Floral Arranging

Silks & Other Artificials

Dried Naturals

Wreaths,
Swags & More

Floral
Accessories

FLORAL ARRANGING

Floral arrangements range from traditional table centerpieces to free-form wall swags to whimsical accessories. Whether made of silk or dried materials or a combination of both, they add color and help soften the lines of a room.

Arrangements can complement any decorating scheme. As accents in a room, arrangements can be enjoyed all year long or used as seasonal displays. Create a harvest basket for the kitchen, a floral centerpiece for the dining room, a wreath for the living room, or a garland for the bedroom.

When making a floral arrangement, consider where it will be placed when it is finished. Decide whether it will be seen from all sides or be placed against a wall or other surface. Select an arrangement style that suits your personal taste, and choose flowers and a container to complement the surrounding decorating scheme. Use either silk or dried floral materials, depending on the look you want to achieve.

Create floral accessories from leftover floral materials. Decorate picture frames, baskets, chandeliers, and wire forms, or make pomanders to hang in a window or fill a decorative basket. For added flair at the dining table, decorate a goblet, place card, or serving tray with flowers and foliage.

BASIC ARRANGEMENT FORMS

Floral arrangements generally follow a basic shape or geometric form. Arrangement forms range from triangular to linear to round. Several of the most common are shown here. The basic forms can be followed exactly, or they may be varied to suit your personal style preferences.

Fan arrangement *contains floral materials that radiate from a central point to form a semicircle.*

Oval arrangement *contains floral materials that outline and fill in either a horizontal or vertical oval shape.*

Crescent arrangement *contains floral materials that curve into a soft crescent shape.*

Horizontal arrangement *is usually low and follows a long horizontal line. The line may contain a slight arc.*

L-shape arrangement *forms a 90° angle at the base. The L shape may be reversed, if desired.*

Round arrangement *contains floral materials that outline and fill in the shape of a sphere. These arrangements are often used as centerpieces, because they look the same from all sides.*

Triangular arrangement *(right) contains floral materials that form a triangle. The shape of the triangle may vary from high and narrow to low and wide.*

Vertical arrangement *is a tall, slender linear design.*

Parallel arrangement *contains two or more vertical groupings of floral materials, sometimes with space between them. The materials may be of varied or uniform heights.*

S-curve arrangement *contains floral materials that form a graceful S shape.*

FLORAL DESIGN

The basic elements of design are line, form, texture, and color. All these elements need to be considered to make an arrangement with good design that fits well into the room. You may choose to repeat elements from the room's decorating scheme in the arrangement. For example, a tall, vertical arrangement with a smooth ceramic vase is suitable for a room with tall, narrow windows and a dramatic decorating scheme.

For a floral arrangement, choose colors that complement or contrast with the colors of the room. To prevent the arrangement from blending in too much, use colors that are slightly lighter or darker than the room colors rather than an exact match.

Design principles such as balance and proportion are also important considerations. These principles are discussed on pages 10 and 11.

LINE

FORM

Form describes the basic shape of an arrangement (pages 6 and 7). In controlled design, the floral materials stay within the boundaries of the shape. In free-form design, the materials fall outside the boundaries to add visual interest.

TEXTURE

Line describes the directional movement in an arrangement. The line of an arrangement may be straight or curved.

Texture helps create the mood of a design. Smooth surfaces can look elegant; rough textures, more rustic. Consider the texture of both the floral materials and the container.

COLOR

Single color can be used for the entire arrangement. Different shades of a color can be used to achieve contrast.

Neighboring colors on the color wheel harmonize, because they contain the same underlying color. For example, red-orange, red, and red-violet all contain the color red.

Evenly spaced colors on the color wheel can be combined for contrast.

Opposite colors on the color wheel can be combined to achieve strong contrast.

BALANCE

When an arrangement has good balance, the flowers are correctly positioned and secured in the container. This not only keeps the arrangement from falling over, but makes it visually pleasing as well. Visual balance is achieved when an arrangement looks balanced to the eye, as in the symmetrical and asymmetrical arrangements below.

Symmetrical balance is achieved by placing flowers in the container so, when an arrangement is divided down the center, it has two halves that look alike. Symmetrical designs are always visually balanced, because the placement of flowers on both sides is the same, or nearly the same.

Asymmetrical balance is achieved by placing flowers in the container so that when an arrangement is divided down the center, it has two halves that look different. However, the design is visually balanced, because the visual weight of both sides is the same.

VISUAL WEIGHT

When an arrangement is visually balanced, the visual weight of the flowers is distributed evenly. Visually, each flower in an arrangement has a certain amount of weight, or emphasis. This is partially determined by the flower's size and color. To achieve a balanced design, consider the information below as you position the flowers in an arrangement.

Size of a flower affects its visual weight. Large flowers have more visual weight than small flowers; however, several small flowers can be grouped together to achieve the visual weight of one large flower.

Color affects the visual weight of a flower. A light-colored flower has less visual weight than a dark-colored flower of the same size. It may take two or more light-colored flowers to give the visual weight of one dark flower.

Similarity of line, size, texture, and color makes the visual weight of one floral material equal to that of another. When similar materials are substituted for one another, the arrangement retains its visual balance.

HARMONY & CONTRAST

Harmony and contrast are used together for a unified floral arrangement that works well in its surroundings. Harmony is created when the arrangement uses elements that are similar to the surroundings, so the arrangement seems to belong where it is placed. Contrast is created when the arrangement uses elements that are different from the surroundings; this prevents the arrangement from blending into the room and gives it more impact.

Harmony exists when elements from the surroundings are repeated in the arrangement. For example, the soft colors in this arrangement blend with the room's color scheme. The shiny surface of the mirror and the glass container with marbles both have reflective qualities. And the white, dainty florets of hydrangea repeat the color and texture of the lace table runner.

Contrast exists when elements of the floral arrangement vary from the surroundings. For example, the majority of the colors in this arrangement are dark, to contrast with the light surroundings. The texture of the arrangement contrasts with the smooth finishes of the pillows and tabletop. The angular lines of the container contrast with the soft lines of the upholstery.

PROPORTION & SCALE

Proportion and scale are important considerations in making a floral arrangement that is suitable for its setting. For good proportion, the size and quantity of the flowers should relate to the size of the container. For correct scale, the arrangement is of a size appropriate for the location.

Proportion and scale relate the size and quantity of the floral materials to the container and relate the size of the arrangement to the setting. For example, the horizontal line of the arrangement works well on the rectangular table, and its height does not interfere with conversation. The arrangement is in correct scale with the goblets and dinnerware.

MAKING A BASIC ARRANGEMENT

In addition to the elements and principles of design, there are general guidelines for the placement of floral materials in an arrangement. The largest and darkest flowers in an arrangement are usually placed near the base of the design, and the smallest and lightest flowers are placed at the outer edges. In symmetrical arrangements, the floral materials are spaced evenly throughout; in asymmetrical arrangements, the floral materials are placed so the visual weight is distributed evenly throughout.

DOMINANT, SECONDARY, FILLER & LINE MATERIALS

Dominant materials are the largest materials in an arrangement. They are usually inserted after the line materials.

Secondary materials are smaller than the dominant materials and are used to finish shaping the form of the design. They are inserted after the dominant materials.

Filler materials usually consist of small flowers or foliage. Used to fill in any of the bare areas throughout the arrangement, the filler materials are the last items that are inserted.

Line materials are used to give line direction to the arrangement. Including flowers, foliage, or twigs, they are usually inserted first to establish the height and width of the arrangement.

HOW TO MAKE A BASIC ARRANGEMENT

1 Select floral materials, and determine the quantity needed by making a bouquet in hand. Check size and color relationships of materials, and determine if size of bouquet is appropriate for the container.

2 Select a basic form (pages 6 and 7), such as round, for the arrangement. Insert foam into container, and cover (page 23). Insert the line material into the foam to establish the height and the width of the selected form.

3 Insert the dominant flowers into arrangement, spacing them evenly and staying within the shape of the desired form.

4 Insert secondary flowers into arrangement, spacing them evenly and staying within the shape of the desired form.

5 Insert filler materials to fill in any bare areas of the desired form.

6 Add an element of interest, such as ivy, if desired, allowing the material to extend outside the basic form.

CONTAINERS

Containers are an integral part of a floral arrangement, often as important to the total design as the flowers themselves. When choosing a container, consider the color, texture, line direction, and size of the arrangement. Also consider where the arrangement will be placed so both the flowers and the container complement the surrounding decorating scheme.

The most common floral container is the vase. However, a variety of other containers can usually be found among kitchen cookware and serving pieces. Look around the kitchen for teapots, water pitchers, serving bowls, and other items made of glass, china, ceramic, or metal. All of these can make suitable containers for floral arrangements. An elegant serving bowl may be appropriate for a formal holiday arrangement, while an old teapot may be perfect for a dried arrangement in a country dining room. For garden-style arrangements, or for designs with a rustic look, select a basket, terra-cotta pot, or wooden box. Many containers can fit into any decorating scheme.

Country containers (right) are often made of natural materials and include items such as thatched and reed baskets and terra-cotta pots. Old watering cans, wire baskets, and pottery pitchers also fit well into this decorating style.

Contemporary containers (below) have simple shapes and clean lines. Use glass or ceramic vases, terra-cotta pots, and metal containers with minimal detailing to accent contemporary arrangements and interiors.

Traditional containers are often elegant and refined. Metal containers, such as a silver teapot or a gold-plated candy dish, work well in traditional interiors. Many porcelain, cut-glass, and ceramic vases are also traditional in style.

TOOLS & SUPPLIES

A number of basic tools and supplies are available at floral shops and craft stores. Those that follow are the most widely used.

A few basic cutting tools, adhesives, wires, and pins are helpful for floral arranging. Floral foam (page 18) is used to hold floral materials in place; the type you select depends upon whether silk or dried materials are used. Moss (page 18) is frequently used to cover the floral foam. Various finishes (page 19) may be used to change the appearance of the floral materials, and dried materials can be protected with an aerosol floral sealer.

CUTTING TOOLS

A heavy-duty wire cutter is used for cutting floral wire, floral stems, and grapevine.

A serrated knife is used for cutting floral Styrofoam® for silk arranging and floral foam for dried arranging.

Scissors are used for cutting the ends of ribbons. Old silk flowers can be revived by trimming frayed edges with scissors.

ADHESIVES

A glue gun and glue sticks **(a)** are used together to secure materials to a base. A glue stick is inserted into an electric glue gun, which melts it. Hot glue can be used to secure floral foam for dried arranging to the bottom of certain containers, such as baskets and terracotta pots. However, it causes floral Styrofoam (page 18) to melt.

Floral tape **(b)** is a narrow tape on a roll and is usually green in color. Made from wax and paper, it is used to cover wires and floral stems.

Thick white craft glue **(c)** can be used for securing flower petals and leaves to floral Styrofoam or other bases.

Floral adhesive clay **(d)** is used for securing floral Styrofoam for silk arranging to a base. It will not adhere to floral foam for dried arranging.

WIRES & PINS

Floral pins **(a),** sometimes called U or S pins, are used to secure moss or other floral materials to foam or straw bases.

Stem wire **(b)** is used to extend the length of floral stems and to bind floral materials together. It is sized by gauge, ranging from 16 to 28. The smaller the number, the thicker the wire.

Floral picks **(c)** are used to extend the length of floral stems and add stems to artificial fruit (page 24).

Paddle floral wire **(d),** usually thin to medium in gauge, is wrapped around a paddle. It is used when long lengths of wire are necessary.

Anchor pins **(e)** are small plastic holders, used to hold floral foam in place. Anchor pins are secured to the container using floral adhesive clay.

MOSSES

Sheet moss **(a)** comes in dried sheets and is used for covering the floral foam in arrangements. It can also be used decoratively to cover a container or wreath base.

Spanish moss **(b)** is used to cover the foam in arrangements. It can be secured to the foam with floral pins.

Reindeer moss **(c)** has a spongy texture. It is added to a finished arrangement for visual interest.

Excelsior **(d)** is added to an arrangement for texture and for visual interest. These curled wood shavings are available bleached or unbleached.

FLORAL FOAMS

Floral Styrofoam® for silk arranging **(a)** is available in sheet form, in green or white, and is used to hold and stabilize floral materials in a silk arrangement. It is available in preshaped forms, such as balls, cones, and eggs, which can be used for making topiaries or pomanders. It is also available in various wreath forms.

Floral foam for dried arranging **(b)** is grayish brown and usually comes in a block. It is used to hold and stabilize dried floral materials in an arrangement.

FINISHES

Aerosol paint (a) can be applied to pinecones, foliage, branches, and pods to change their colors or to add a metallic finish.

Acrylic paint (b) can be brushed on leaves, flower petals, and dried or artificial fruit to add visual interest and color contrast.

Aerosol floral sealer (c) can be applied to dried materials to help prevent shattering.

Wax-based paint (d) can be rubbed onto floral materials to give a metallic finish.

WORK AREA & STORAGE

Although dried and silk flowers can be arranged almost anywhere, kitchen counters and tables usually provide good work areas. Work near an electrical outlet if using a glue gun. Because it can be messy to work with moss and dried materials, cover the work surface with newspaper, and keep a large trash can nearby. For convenience, use a sheet of Styrofoam® to hold floral pins, picks, anchor pins, and stem wire.

When working on an arrangement, place it so it will be arranged at the same height from which it will be viewed when displayed. Or, during arranging, place the arrangement in its final location occasionally, to check the placement of the floral materials. When working on larger projects, such as garlands, allow plenty of room, so the entire project fits on the work surface.

Store silk floral materials upright; they can become flattened or wrinkled if they are stored flat. Keep them out of direct sunlight to prevent fading. Store dried floral materials by hanging them upside down from hooks or by laying them on crumpled tissue paper and storing them in cardboard boxes. To prevent dried materials from fading and molding, keep them in a location that is dark, dry, and well ventilated.

TIPS FOR THE WORK AREA

Pegboard can be convenient for holding a wall swag while you arrange it. This allows you to see how the swag will look when it is displayed. The pegboard is also helpful for keeping floral tape, ribbons, and cutting tools within easy reach.

Cardboard box is used to elevate a centerpiece to the same height as its final display location. This makes it easier to achieve balance and even distribution of floral materials.

TIPS FOR STORAGE

Silk materials are easily stored by placing floral Styrofoam® in the bottom of a cardboard box and inserting flowers upright into the foam. Cover the box with dark plastic to prevent the materials from fading.

Dried floral materials are stored by hanging them in bunches from a dowel. Flower heads are stored in a cardboard box and cushioned with tissue paper. A small amount of silica gel (page 67) may be placed in the bottom of the box, to absorb any moisture. Flat floral materials, such as mosses and leaves, are stored by laying them on crumpled newspaper in a cardboard box.

PREPARING FLORAL FOAM

Floral foam for silk and dried arrangements can be secured to the container in several ways, depending on the type of foam and the type of container being used.

Floral foam is used as a holding device to secure and stabilize flowers in an arrangement. Floral Styrofoam® is sturdy foam designed for use with silk and artificial floral materials; it comes in a variety of shapes and is usually green or white. Dried floral materials are fragile and therefore require a soft floral foam to prevent stems from breaking when they are inserted. Floral foam appropriate for dried arranging is grayish brown and usually comes in block form.

Floral foam can be secured to containers in several ways, depending on the type of foam and the container being used. The simplest method is to wedge the foam tightly into the container to prevent the foam from shifting.

Floral foam for dried arranging can be secured to many containers, using hot glue. Avoid gluing foam pieces together, because the glued area hardens, making it difficult to insert the stems, and forcing stems could cause breakage. Floral adhesive clay does not stick to floral foam for dried arranging. In order to use floral foam for dried arranging with floral adhesive clay, you must secure an anchor pin to the bottom of the container, using floral adhesive clay. Then insert the floral foam into the container over the anchor pin.

Floral Styrofoam for silk arranging can be secured to most containers using floral adhesive clay. Hot glue is usually avoided, because it melts Styrofoam; when hot glue is used, allow the glued surface to cool slightly before placing it in direct contact with the Styrofoam.

The height of the foam in an arrangement depends on whether the arrangement is vertical or horizontal, and whether the floral stems are flexible. For vertical floral arrangements, the foam usually falls ½" to ¾" (1.3 to 2 cm) below the rim of the container. For horizontal or draping arrangements, the foam is usually even with or extends above the rim. Less flexible stems require foam that extends to about 1" (2.5 cm) above the container. This makes it easier to position floral materials outward or downward near the rim.

PREPARING FLORAL FOAM FOR NONGLASS CONTAINERS

1 Vertical floral arrangement.
Select appropriate type of floral foam for a dried or silk arrangement. Cut foam, using knife, so it fits container snugly and is ½" to ¾" (1.3 to 2 cm) below rim; cut and insert wedges of foam as necessary.

2 Cover foam lightly with moss, securing it with floral pins, if necessary.

1 Horizontal or draping floral arrangement.
Select appropriate type of floral foam for a dried or silk arrangement. Cut the foam, using knife, so it fits the container snugly and is even with or extends about 1" (2.5 cm) above container, depending on flexibility of the floral stems. Round off the top edges of foam, if necessary, to prevent foam from showing in finished arrangement.

2 Cover foam lightly with moss, securing it with floral pins, if necessary.

PREPARING FLORAL FOAM FOR GLASS CONTAINERS

Silk floral arrangement.
Cut floral Styrofoam so it can be inserted into center of the container with space around all sides. Apply floral adhesive clay to bottom of foam; secure to bottom of container. Fill surrounding area with potpourri, marbles, small pinecones, or other desired material.

Dried floral arrangement. Cut block of floral foam so it can be inserted into the center of container with space around all sides. Apply floral adhesive clay to the bottom of anchor pin; secure to the bottom of glass container. Press the foam firmly onto prongs of anchor pin. Fill surrounding area with marbles, potpourri, small pinecones, or other desired material.

FLORAL TIPS & TECHNIQUES

Add wire stems **(a)** to artificial fruits and vegetables by inserting heavy stem wire into fruit and securing with hot glue; conceal the wire with floral tape. Or add floral picks **(b)** to fruits and vegetables by making a small hole in fruit with an awl; insert a pick into hole, securing it with hot glue.

Gild floral materials, such as leaves, artichokes, and pinecones, with metallic aerosol paint.

Add stems to pinecones by wrapping stem wire around bottom layers of the pinecone, twisting to secure. Wrap wire with floral tape before securing to pinecones, if desired.

Add flexibility to dried floral stems by placing stem wire against natural stem and wrapping the two together with floral tape.

Brush acrylic paints onto floral petals or leaves to accent them or to give dimension to the materials.

Extend lengths of floral stems by placing stem wire against stem; secure together, using floral tape **(a).** Or wire the stems to wooden picks **(b).**

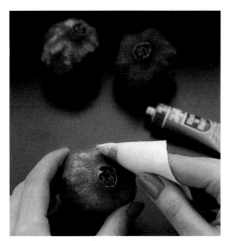

Rub gold wax-based paint onto floral materials, such as pomegranates, to add highlights.

Bend and shape the leaves and petals of artificial floral materials for a more natural appearance.

Highlight twigs or other floral materials with glitter, frost, or aerosol paint.

Glue wire stems to flower heads, using a hot glue gun. Conceal wire by wrapping it with floral tape.

Protect fragile dried floral materials from shattering by spraying them with an aerosol floral sealer.

Clean dried floral materials and hand-wrapped silk materials by using a hair dryer to blow away dust.

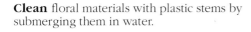

Clean floral materials with plastic stems by submerging them in water.

Silks & Other
Artificials

SILK FLOWERS

Silk is the general term used to describe any artificial floral materials, including those made of silk, polyester, parchment, or latex. Silk flowers usually have wired stems, making them flexible; the wire stems are covered with floral tape or plastic. Flowers with plastic stems are more economical. Silk flowers are available at most floral shops, garden centers, and craft stores.

Ranunculus

Anthurium

Daisy

Wild rose

Iris

Statice

Miniature roses

Larkspur

Delphinium

Forsythia

Hydrangeas

Baby's breath

Peony

Gingerroot heliconia

Freesia

Sunflower

Alstroemeria

Begonia

Bird of paradise

Rose

Sweet william

Lilac

Astilbe

SILK FOLIAGE,
BERRIES & FRUIT

Leafy silk, or artificial, foliage is available in a variety
of shapes and colors. Artificial berries and fruit, often
of latex, papier-mâché, or plastic, are available in
clusters, attached to vines, and as
individual items.

*Marsh
berries*

Ginkgo

Ivy

*Autumn
foliage*

Begonia

Pumpkin vine

Bear
grass

Caladium

Rose hip

Grapes

Pear

SINGLE-VARIETY ARRANGEMENTS

A single variety of flowers, displayed in a vase, makes a simple arrangement with dramatic impact. Several blossoms in one color can be stunning. To achieve the look of fresh-cut flowers, display the arrangement in a clear glass container.

HOW TO MAKE A SINGLE-VARIETY ARRANGEMENT

MATERIALS

- Silk irises or other flowers.
- Clear glass container.
- Clear marbles.

- Floral Styrofoam® for silk arranging.
- Floral adhesive clay.
- Wire cutter; serrated knife.

1 Insert floral Styrofoam for silk arranging into glass container; cover with marbles (page 23).

2 Insert flowers into foam, spacing evenly around container and varying heights. Bend stems slightly downward near outer edges for natural appearance.

Single stems, each in its own vase, are grouped together for impact.

MORE IDEAS FOR SINGLE-VARIETY ARRANGEMENTS

Several colors *of a single variety make a bold statement when placed in a colorful, artistic vase.*

Artificial bulbs *are placed in specially designed glass vases. Crocus flowers are inserted into the bulbs for a realistic look.*

SILK CENTERPIECES

Centerpieces are designed to be seen from all sides and are therefore usually symmetrical in shape. Made from silk materials, centerpieces may be seasonal displays of color or they may be used year-round. They can vary in height or size, depending on their intended use. Low arrangements are ideal on a dining room table, while taller arrangements create a dramatic display on a sofa table or pedestal.

HOW TO MAKE A SILK CENTERPIECE

MATERIALS

- Silk roses or other dominant flowers.
- Silk rosebuds or other secondary flowers.
- Silk sweet william or other filler flowers.
- Marsh berries or other filler material.
- Silk begonia or other flowering leafy plant.

- Brass pot or other container.
- Floral Styrofoam® for silk arranging.
- Spanish moss.
- Wire cutter; serrated knife.
- Floral pins.

1 Insert foam into container, and cover (page 23). Insert roses into foam, spacing them evenly. Bend stems and leaves as necessary to give flowers a natural appearance.

2 Cut begonia plant apart at base of stems, using wire cutter. Extend length of stems with wire or picks as necessary (page 24); insert into arrangement, spacing evenly.

3 Insert rosebuds evenly throughout arrangement so the centerpiece appears balanced from all angles.

4 Cut sweet william stems to desired lengths; insert flowers evenly into arrangement to fill in any bare areas.

5 Insert the stems of marsh berries evenly. Adjust flowers or leaves to balance the design and give a natural appearance.

THREE-SIDED
SILK ARRANGEMENTS

Three-sided arrangements are designed to be used against a wall or in a corner of a room. Use silk flowers and foliage to create the triangular design shown here, following the instructions below. Or make any of the other basic arrangements on pages 6 and 7 by inserting the materials as necessary to achieve the desired form.

HOW TO MAKE A THREE-SIDED SILK ARRANGEMENT

MATERIALS

- Silk daisies or other dominant flowers.
- Silk ranunculus and grape hyacinth or other secondary flowers.
- Silk desert candle or other filler flowers.
- Silk variegated ivy or other foliage.

- Silk forsythia or other line material.
- Brass pot or other container.
- Floral Styrofoam® for silk arranging.
- Wire cutter; serrated knife; floral pins.

1 Insert foam into container, and cover (page 23). Insert forsythia into foam, placing one tall stem in center and one short stem on each side to establish height and width. Adjust length of stems, if desired.

2 Continue inserting forsythia, and insert ivy into the arrangement, creating desired shape; place some of the materials at the back. Materials in the center point upward, and materials on the sides point outward.

3 Insert daisies into arrangement, spacing evenly throughout to keep arrangement balanced on three sides.

4 Insert ranunculus and grape hyacinth evenly, one variety at a time, so the arrangement appears balanced.

5 Insert desert candle into arrangement to fill in any bare areas.

S-CURVE ARRANGEMENTS

An asymmetrical S-curve arrangement can be viewed from three sides, and therefore works well placed against a wall or in a corner. The design is formed by shaping the silk line material into an S form. Dominant flowers are inserted within the curved design, then bare areas filled in with filler flowers and foliage to complete the arrangement.

HOW TO MAKE AN S-CURVE ARRANGEMENT

MATERIALS

- Silk delphinium or other line material.
- Silk roses or other dominant flowers.
- Silk statice and hydrangeas or other filler flowers.
- Tall vase or other container.
- Floral Styrofoam® for silk arranging.
- Spanish moss.
- Wire cutter; serrated knife.
- Floral pins.

1 Insert foam in container, and cover with moss (page 23). Insert the silk delphinium, placing some on the left side, pointing upward, and some on right side, draping downward. Shape stems into an S shape.

2 Cut one rose stem short, placing it in the center toward front of the container; trim off any excess leaves; set aside. Insert the remaining roses, bending the stems as necessary to maintain the desired S shape.

3 Insert the stems of hydrangeas to fill in the S shape. Longer stems curve upward on left side and downward on right; stems of flowers in the center are cut short to maintain the shape of the design.

4 Insert the statice, spacing evenly along curve. Tuck any remaining leaves into the center of the arrangement to fill any bare areas. Bend the stems as necessary to maintain the S shape.

MORE IDEAS FOR SILK ARRANGEMENTS

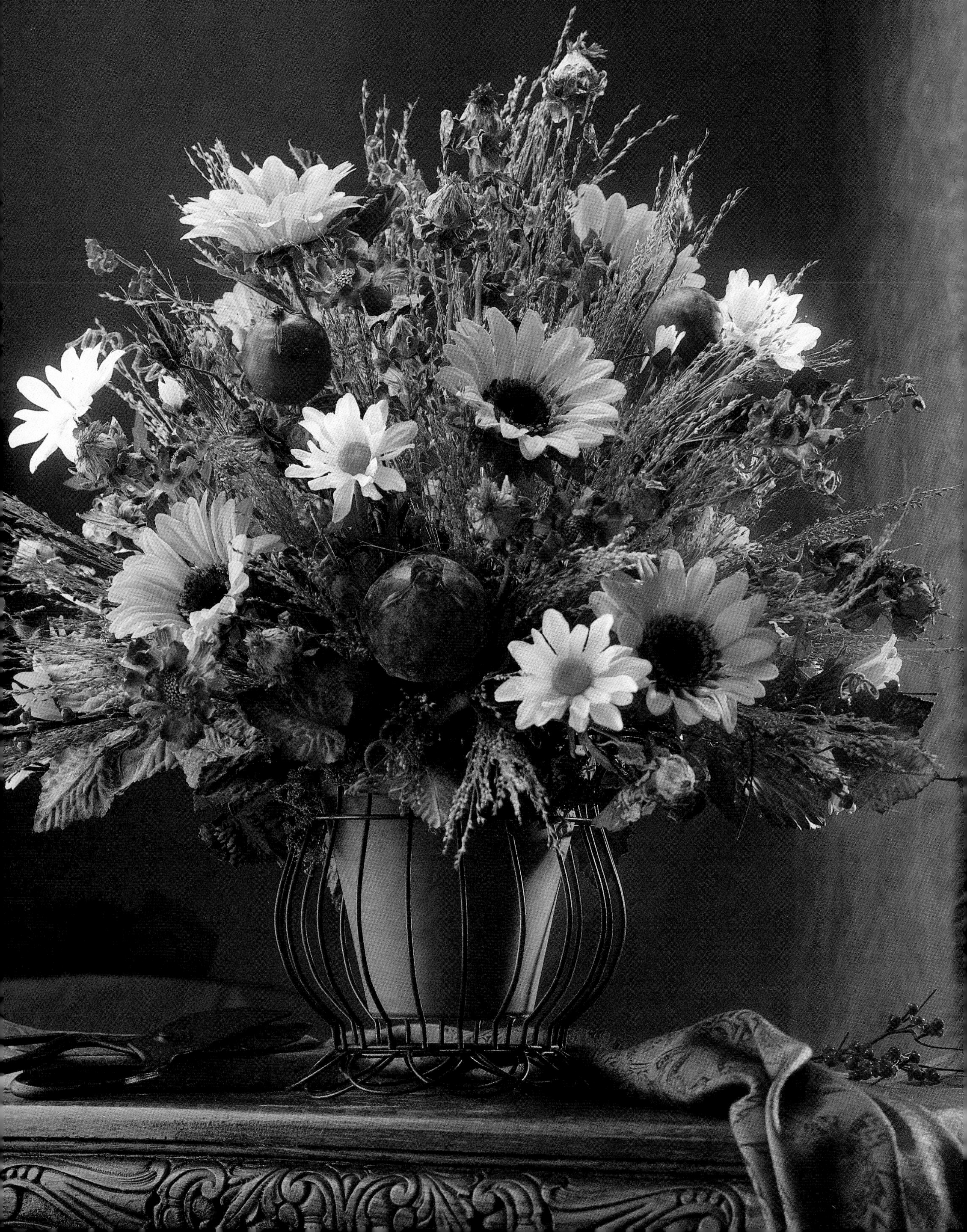

Autumn colors *dominate the floral arrangement opposite, which combines both silk and dried floral materials for textural interest. The rustic look is emphasized by the terra-cotta and wire container.*

Opposite colors *on the color wheel are used to create a dramatic display in the elegant vase at right. Silk ranunculus, snapdragons, and irises are combined with dried Queen Anne's lace.*

Spring colors *are used in the crescent arrangement below. Line materials are shaped to give the design its form.*

TROPICAL ARRANGEMENTS

Tropical flowers make a dramatic statement. Although usually arranged asymmetrically as shown here, tropical arrangements are occasionally symmetrical (page 47). Tropical arrangements often complement contemporary interiors; however, small arrangements can be suitable for other decorating styles, and a party may be an excellent opportunity to use tropical silk flowers as a decorating accent.

HOW TO MAKE AN ASYMMETRICAL TROPICAL ARRANGEMENT

MATERIALS

- Silk gingerroot heliconia, birds of paradise, and anthurium or other dominant flowers.
- Silk ti leaves, variegated plants, and caladium plants or other foliage.
- Dried lotus pods or other pods.

- Low container.
- Floral Styrofoam® for silk arranging.
- Spanish moss.
- Wire cutter; serrated knife; floral pins.

1 Insert foam into container, and cover (page 23). Insert two ti leaves on right side and two on the left; insert one into center, pointing upward. Shape leaves as desired.

2 Insert some variegated leaves into center to give height, and insert additional stems in the front and on the right. Insert caladium leaves around the rim to fill in any bare areas.

3 Group flowers by variety to make each more noticeable, placing the gingerroot heliconia in center at varying heights and anthurium on the right side.

4 Cut two bird of paradise stems short; insert on left side at the front of container. Place one in the center, keeping height about the same as gingerroot heliconia. Insert lotus pods cut to varying heights on the right side of arrangement to add texture and visual weight.

MORE IDEAS FOR TROPICAL ARRANGEMENTS

Tropical varieties *in burgundy and white are mixed with bear grass and plumosa, to make an elegant arrangement. They are placed in a gold mesh vase that has been decorated with a matching cord and tassels.*

Large tropicals *(right) in orange and red are used together for bold impact. Combine birds of paradise, protea, and gingerroot heliconia to create this dramatic display.*

Orchids (left) are arranged vertically in a glass vase. The design is softened by adding curly willow and bear grass. Because of the symmetrical shape and the cut-glass vase, this arrangement works well in a traditional room.

Mixed tropicals including anthurium, devil's claw heliconia, birds of paradise, and orchids are combined for a dramatic asymmetrical design. Curly willow is added for visual interest.

HARVEST BASKETS

Harvest baskets, traditionally used in the autumn to gather nature's bounty, are re-created with silk flowers and latex fruit. A harvest basket complements any interior, from traditional to contemporary to country, mixing flowers and foliage with other desired elements.

Floral materials can easily be changed to reflect the current season or holiday. Place a traditional harvest basket on a fireplace hearth, or create a seasonal display for a kitchen or dining area.

MATERIALS

- Silk sunflowers or other dominant flowers.
- Silk roses and rosebuds or other secondary flowers.
- Silk begonia or other leafy plant.
- Silk autumn foliage and ginkgo or other filler materials.
- Two clusters of artificial apples or other large fruit measuring 1½" to 2½" (3.8 to 6.5 cm) in diameter.

- Five clusters of artificial grapes, to balance apples.
- Several 20" (51 cm) lengths of honeysuckle vine.
- Hickory bark basket with handle, about 12" × 15" (30.5 × 38 cm).
- Floral Styrofoam® for silk arranging.
- Spanish moss.
- Wire cutter; serrated knife; floral pins.

HOW TO MAKE A HARVEST BASKET

1 Insert foam in container, and cover (page 23). Wrap honeysuckle vines around basket, and insert ends into foam.

2 Cut sunflower stems with a wire cutter so flowers stair-step in height from top of basket handle to rim. Insert sunflowers on left side, with tallest stems to the left of center and shorter ones near the outside.

3 Add floral picks to fruit (page 24). Insert apples on right side toward front of basket, and insert central stem of begonia plant into center. Allow plant stems to cascade between other items.

4 Cut all rosebuds to the same height; insert them evenly on right side of arrangement. Bend and shape stems and leaves for a natural appearance.

5 Insert grape clusters on the left side, allowing them to cascade over front of basket. Cut rose stems, and insert in diagonal line on left side.

6 Cut foliage to desired lengths, and insert into bare areas of arrangement.

MORE IDEAS FOR HARVEST BASKETS

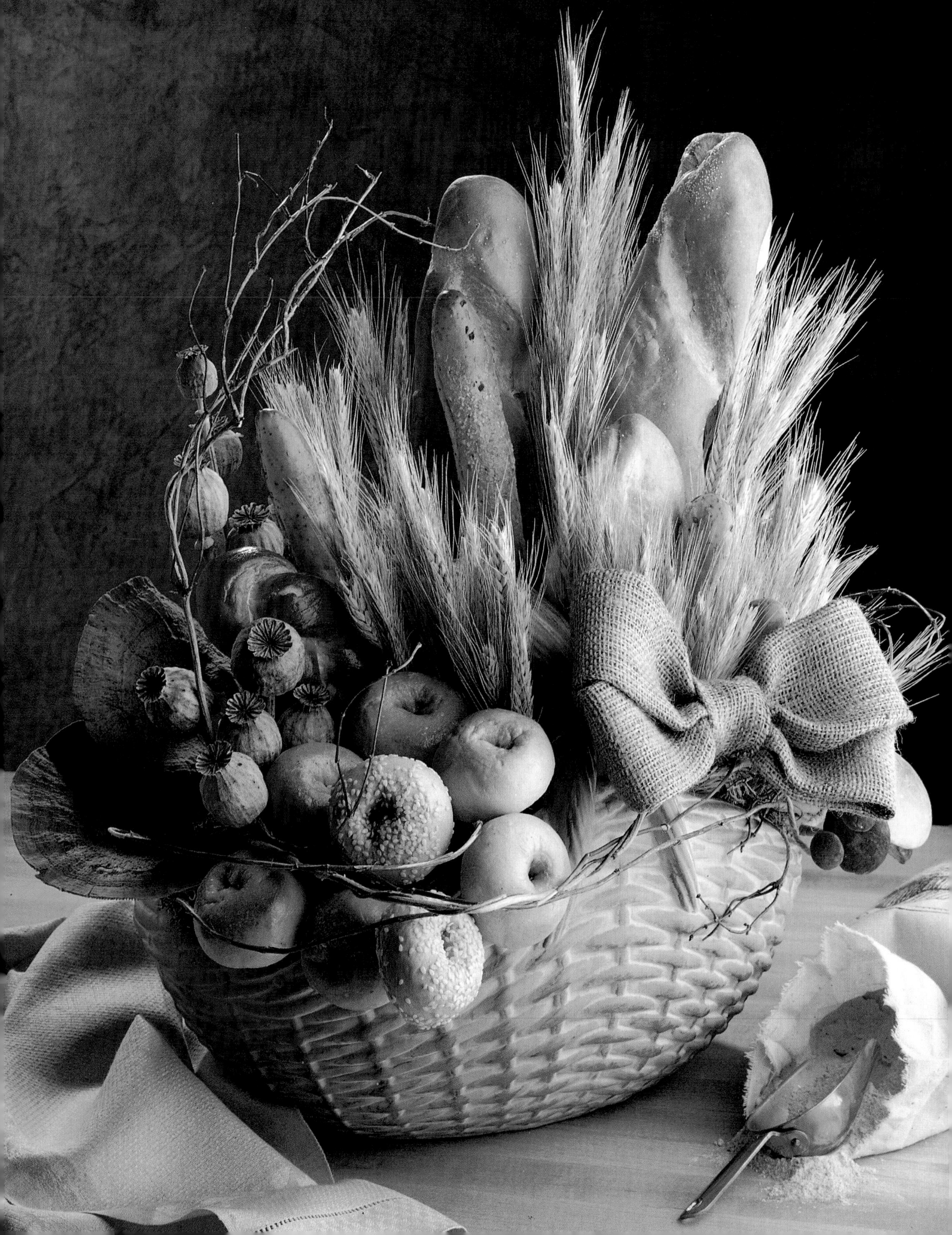

Holiday basket *features poinsettia as the dominant flowers, with artificial berries and chestnuts extending over the sides of the basket. A gold and green bow ties together the gilded walnuts (page 24) and the green sprigs of cedar and holly. Twigs are used as line material.*

Spring basket *has clustered spring flowers. A craft bird and several nests are used as accents. The artificial eggs are covered with flower petals as on page 119.*

Kitchen basket *(opposite) is filled with decorative breads, wheat, poppy pods, and mushrooms. The breads are coated with an aerosol acrylic sealer. Honeysuckle vines and a burlap bow are used as accents.*

Vegetable basket *(right) displays an array of garden vegetables. Vines of squash flowers twist around the basket handle. Pea pods are draped on the left, and squash hangs over the edge of the basket.*

FRUIT BASKETS

Fruit baskets are traditional arrangements that make excellent centerpieces in the dining room or kitchen. They are perfect arrangements for informal settings. Use seasonal elements, or pick up a color or theme that coordinates with the decorating scheme of a room. For easy arranging, purchase latex, plastic, or papier-mâché fruit on wire or wooden stems. Or add your own stems to artificial fruit, using stem wire or wooden picks (page 24).

HOW TO MAKE A FRUIT BASKET

MATERIALS

- Fruits such as apples, plums, pomegranates, grapes, pears, nectarines, and cherries on wire or wooden stems.
- Silk pumpkin vines or other leafy foliage.
- Basket.
- Floral Styrofoam® for silk arranging.

- Spanish moss, sheet moss, or a combination of both.
- 16-gauge floral wire and floral tape; or wooden picks and awl if fruit is not prewired.
- Wire cutter; serrated knife; floral pins.
- Hot glue gun and glue sticks.

1 Insert foam in basket (page 23). Cover foam with Spanish moss, sheet moss, or a combination of both; combine mosses to give a more textured and natural look.

2 Add picks or wire to fruit, if necessary (page 24). Separate fruit by variety and by color. Select color that dominates, such as purple, and insert largest items first, one variety at a time; allow grapes to drape over edges of basket. Set aside smallest purple items to insert later. Check the arrangement for balance after each variety is inserted.

3 Select second most dominant color, such as red, and insert fruit evenly throughout the basket, one variety at a time; set aside the smallest red items to insert later.

4 Repeat step 3 with remaining fruit, spacing evenly throughout. Check arrangement from all sides for balance.

5 Place the smallest items into basket to fill in bare areas and to balance color throughout arrangement. Insert pumpkin vine to fill in remaining bare areas and to soften design. Bend and shape stems to give a natural appearance.

Wire basket (above) combines apples, grapes, pinecones, and nuts in a festive display. Seeded eucalyptus is used as filler.

Ceramic urn (opposite) replaces the traditional basket for a classic fruit centerpiece. Grape clusters drape over the sides for a dramatic effect. Ivy is used as filler, and honeysuckle vines spiral throughout the arrangement.

Grapevine basket (right) combines summer fruits and melons. The berries are added for textural interest and color contrast.

PLANTSCAPES

Plants and trees provide visual contrast and are often used to soften the lines of a room. Placed in groupings called *plantscapes,* they can make beautiful displays. A single plant, such as an ivy, is effective when draped over a hutch or nestled on a shelf among a grouping of collectibles. Larger plants and trees are used in the corners of a room or fill spaces between furnishings.

Silk plants may be used in areas where it would be difficult to grow live plants, such as beneath a sofa table or on top of an armoire. Silk plants require little maintenance or care. Arrangements or groupings of silk plants can easily be changed from season to season, simply by replacing one plant or flower in a grouping with another.

Ferns (above), are potted identically and used for balance on a mantel.

Seasonal flowers are combined with a variety of leafy silk plants. The plantscape can easily be adapted for other seasons by replacing peonies and geraniums with poinsettias, sunflowers, or daffodils.

Ivy is draped over a hutch to soften the hard edges of the furniture.

Ficus tree (left) is the focus of a floor plantscape. Honeysuckle vines spiral around the tree and are secured with floral wire. Silk plants are arranged at the base of the ficus. An additional potted plant sits near the ficus to complete the plantscape.

Silk houseplants, grouped on a table, help to unify a collection of ceramics.

Dried
Naturals

DRIED FLOWERS & GRAINS

Dried floral materials, sometimes called dried naturals, are natural materials that have been dehydrated, so they will last for long periods of time. When fresh flowers are air dried, they often shrink in size, their colors soften, and they have a more textured appearance. Flowers that are dried in silica gel or that are preserved by freeze drying often retain their original shape, although their colors may change slightly. Dried floral materials are available at many floral shops, garden centers, and craft stores. Or you may dry your own, as on pages 66 to 69.

Pepper grass

Lavender

Wheat

Mixed herbs

Limonium

Leptosporum

Rushes

Strawflowers

Hydrangea

Zinnias

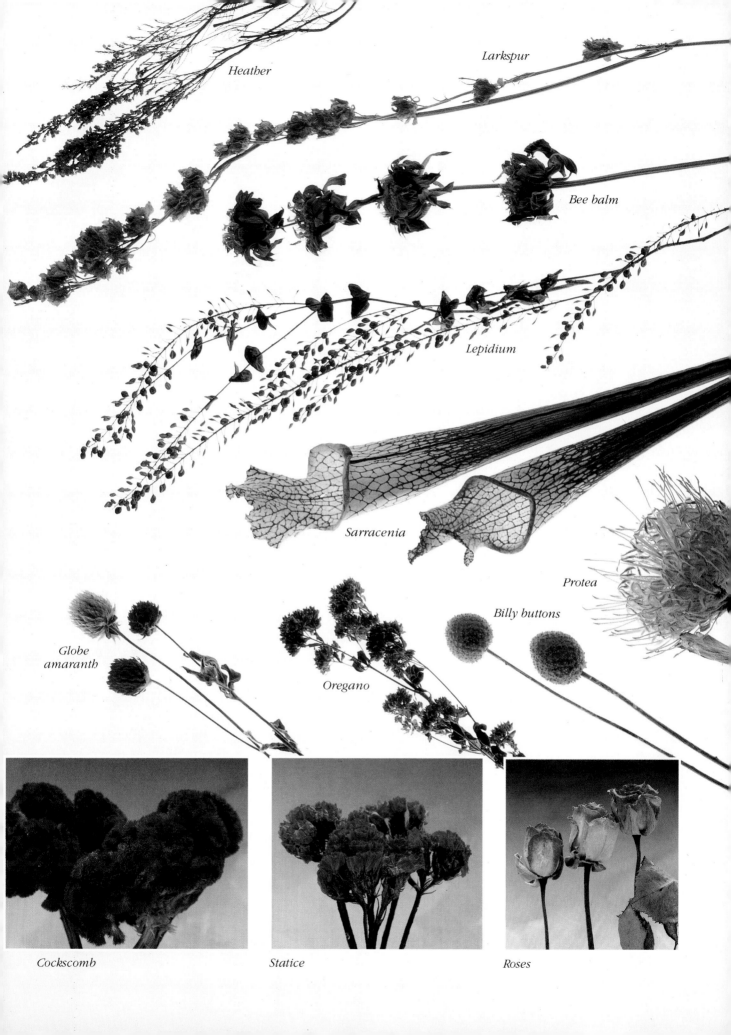

Heather

Larkspur

Bee balm

Lepidium

Sarracenia

Protea

Globe
amaranth

Oregano

Billy buttons

Cockscomb

Statice

Roses

DRIED FOLIAGE

Dried foliage is available in many varieties. Some fresh foliage can be air dried, as on page 68. Other varieties can be preserved in glycerine, which makes them more flexible and less brittle to work with. Dried and preserved foliage is available at many floral shops, garden centers, and craft stores.

Boston fern

Huckleberry with brake fern

Seeded eucalyptus

Galax

Leatherleaf

Spiral eucalyptus

Maidenhair fern

Silver-dollar eucalyptus

Protea

Boxwood

Bear grass

Salal

DRIED BERRIES, PODS & MORE

Many varieties of dried berries, pods, cones, and fruit are available at floral shops, garden centers, and craft stores. You can dry your own materials, as on page 68.

Artichoke

Assorted nuts

Lotus pods

Honeysuckle vines

Garlic bulb

Pepper berries

Poppy pods

Assorted cones

Nigella pods

Canella berries

Pomegranates

DRYING FLOWERS

Limonium

Flax

Delphinium

Caspia

Air drying *on mesh works well for billy buttons, protea, and sunflowers.*

Drying your own floral materials gives you a wider range of materials to work with when making floral arrangements. Floral materials can be air dried or dried in silica gel. Air-dried flowers may be dried with their stems attached; when dry, the flowers will be smaller than their original size, and the petals and leaves will have a wrinkled appearance. Flowers dried in silica gel are dried without their stems; after drying, wire stems may be added (page 24). Flowers dried in silica gel retain the appearance of fresh flowers and remain close to their original shapes and sizes.

AIR DRYING

There are several air-drying methods for floral materials. Most varieties can be dried by hanging them upside down (above). Leaves, branches, mosses, and seed pods are usually dried flat. Some materials, such as ornamental grasses, dry well when they are set upright in a container, allowing them to bend naturally.

Other materials are dried upright in a container with a small amount of water; the water slows the drying time and helps materials retain their shapes and colors. Floral materials with large heads, such as artichokes, protea, and sunflowers, are dried by supporting the heads on wire mesh. Materials that break easily after they are dried, such as heather, boxwood, and salal, can be arranged while they are still fresh and left to dry in the arrangement.

The drying time of floral materials varies, depending on the density of and moisture in the materials, as well as the temperature and humidity of the environment. The drying time can range from a few days to several weeks; most materials dry within five days to two weeks.

When drying floral materials, place them in a location that is dark, dry, and well ventilated. Once dried, they can be stored as on pages 20 and 21.

Liatris   *Mimosa*   *Heather*   *Bachelor's buttons*

Silica-gel drying *works well for peonies, roses, and asters.*

SILICA-GEL DRYING

Available at many floral shops and craft stores, silica gel is a powder that dries flower heads to a nearly fresh appearance within a few days. It absorbs moisture from the flowers while supporting them in their natural shapes. The silica gel can be reused several times.

For best results, select flowers just before they reach full bloom; most flowers dried in full bloom do not retain their colors as well and have a tendency to fall apart when dry. If using flowers from a garden, pick them when they contain the least amount of moisture, usually early in the morning or late in the afternoon. Flowers that are deep pink, orange, yellow, blue, or purple retain their colors well. Red flowers tend to turn black when dry, and pastels and whites may turn brown.

The necessary drying time varies. Flowers with thin petals may dry in two to three days; dense flower heads may take five to seven days. Check the flowers every day while they are drying, so they do not overdry and become brittle.

Flowers dried in silica gel are very fragile. Handle them carefully when making the arrangement, inserting them last whenever possible. Store any extra flowers in a box, as on pages 20 and 21. Place a small amount of silica gel in the bottom of the box to absorb any moisture and keep the flowers dry.

HOW TO AIR DRY FLOWERS

Drying upright without water.
Place branches or grasses in a dry
container; allow to dry.

Drying upright with water. Pour water into
vase to depth of 2" (5 cm). Remove the lower
leaves of floral materials, and place materials
upright in vase; allow to dry. Water evaporates,
leaving flowers preserved.

Drying upright on wire mesh.
Place wire mesh over deep box.
Insert flower stems through mesh,
allowing flower heads to rest on
mesh. Support flower heads with
tissue paper, if necessary.

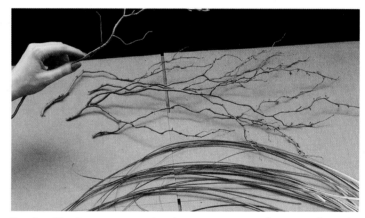

Drying flat. Lay grasses, twigs, leaves, or mosses flat on cardboard
or newspaper; allow to dry. Turn the materials over occasionally,
to ensure even drying.

METHODS FOR AIR DRYING FLOWERS

SUGGESTED METHOD	VARIETIES
DRYING UPRIGHT WITHOUT WATER	Branches; cattails; ornamental grasses; pussy willow; sea lavender.
DRYING UPRIGHT WITH WATER	Baby's breath; bear grass; hybrid delphiniums; hydrangea; mimosa; Queen Anne's lace.
DRYING UPRIGHT ON WIRE MESH	Billy buttons; globe artichokes; peonies; protea; roses; sunflowers.
DRYING UPSIDE DOWN	Bells of Ireland; caspia; globe amaranth; grains; herbs; larkspur; lavender; liatris; mimosa; nigella; peonies; roses; statice.
DRYING FLAT	Bear grass; branches; leaves; mosses; seed pods.

Drying upside down. Select flowers just before
they reach full bloom. Remove lower leaves; trim
damaged areas. Bundle flowers together loosely,
staggering flower heads so air can circulate evenly.
Secure bundle near ends of stems with rubber band;
hang to dry.

HOW TO DRY FLOWERS IN SILICA GEL

MATERIALS

- Flower heads.
- Silica gel; airtight container.
- Newspaper; wire cutter.
- Slotted spoon; soft-bristle paintbrush.

1 Cut stems to within 1" (2.5 cm) of flower heads. Fill container with silica gel, to a depth of 1½" to 2" (3.8 to 5 cm).

2 Place flowers face up in silica gel. Gently sprinkle silica gel between flower petals.

3 Cover flowers completely with silica gel. Cover tightly with lid; allow to dry for two to seven days. Check daily, while drying, so flowers do not overdry and become brittle.

4 Remove flowers from silica gel by tipping container and gently pouring some of the silica gel onto a newspaper. When flowers are visible, gently lift them from silica gel with a slotted spoon.

5 Remove any excess silica gel from the flower petals with a soft brush. Attach any fallen petals with glue. Spray the flowers with aerosol floral sealer (page 19). Dry the silica gel, following manufacturer's directions, so it may be reused.

DRIED CENTERPIECES

Create beautiful centerpieces that fit into a variety of settings, depending on the materials you select. Use delicate dried florals and preserved airy greens for an arrangement with a touch of romance; or use dried pods, cattails, and grains to bring the country indoors.

Centerpieces are usually symmetrical in shape, since they are designed to be seen from all sides. To keep the design balanced, step away from the arrangement occasionally while creating it, and reposition the flowers, if necessary.

HOW TO MAKE A DRIED CENTERPIECE

MATERIALS

- Dried cockscomb and roses or other dominant flowers.
- Dried hydrangeas or other secondary flowers.
- Dried poppy pods and two colors of larkspur or other filler materials.
- Dried lepidium or other line material.
- Preserved maidenhair fern and galax leaves or other foliage.
- Container.
- Floral foam for dried arranging.
- Spanish moss.
- Wire cutter; serrated knife; floral pins.

1 Insert floral foam into container, and cover (page 23). Insert the lepidium into foam, establishing the shape of the arrangement.

2 Insert galax leaves into center to fill in any bare areas. Insert the cockscomb into the arrangement, spacing it evenly throughout.

3 Insert roses, spacing them evenly throughout; add wire to stems, if necessary (page 24). Insert hydrangeas, spacing them evenly throughout, filling in the rounded shape.

4 Insert poppy pods for contrast, spacing them evenly throughout. Insert larkspur, one color at a time, spacing evenly.

5 Insert maidenhair fern to fill in any bare areas; allow it to drape downward slightly.

THREE-SIDED DRIED ARRANGEMENTS

A three-sided arrangement is meant to be placed against a wall or other surface, so only three sides are visible. To preserve the look of fresh flowers, the protea are dried in silica gel as on page 69. Potpourri decoratively fills the space between the clear glass container and the floral foam.

HOW TO MAKE A THREE-SIDED DRIED ARRANGEMENT

MATERIALS

- Dried protea or other dominant flowers.
- Dried billy buttons or other secondary flowers.
- Dried salal, protea leaves, and fern or other dried foliage.
- Curly willow.
- Glass container.
- Floral foam for dried arranging.
- Potpourri; Spanish moss.
- Wire cutter; serrated knife; floral adhesive clay; anchor pin.

1 Insert floral foam into container (page 23); allow space around all sides. Fill area between the foam and the container with potpourri. Sprinkle some potpourri over top of foam.

2 Add wire stems to protea (page 25). Insert protea, then billy buttons, into foam, spacing evenly. Insert taller flowers toward the back and shorter flowers around sides and front.

3 Insert dried foliage, one variety at a time, to fill in any bare areas; keep taller stems toward back. Insert curly willow at back of arrangement to emphasize height. Tuck Spanish moss around rim of container.

MORE IDEAS FOR DRIED ARRANGEMENTS

Watering can *contains a three-sided country arrangement of wheat, eucalyptus, roses, and grapes.*

Garden basket *is created with mixed hydrangeas and stems of larkspur. Bells of Ireland add textural interest to the centerpiece.*

Crystal bowl complements a festive centerpiece of preserved boxwood, cedar, and silver-dollar eucalyptus. Pink roses and pepper berries add color to the arrangement, while pinecones and lotus pods give textural interest. The pinecones are attached to wire stems that have been covered with floral tape.

Brass pot (below) holds dried materials and artificial fruit. Line materials establish the shape of the three-sided design.

Painted metal container contrasts with the bright flowers of the centerpiece. Heather and cockscomb are combined with clusters of roses and globe amaranth.

WALL BASKETS

Wall baskets can be filled with dried line and filler materials. Dominant and secondary flowers may also be added, if desired. You may want to embellish the arrangement with a ribbon or raffia bow.

HOW TO MAKE A WALL BASKET

MATERIALS

- Eucalyptus or other line material.
- Dried roses, strawflowers, globe amaranth, and nigella pods or other filler materials.
- Wall basket.
- Floral foam for dried arranging.
- Sheet moss.
- Wire cutter.
- 22-gauge paddle floral wire.

1 Line basket with moss, if necessary. Cut the foam to fit basket. Insert wire through foam, placing small twig between wire and foam; pull wire through foam to back side.

2 Insert foam into basket. Pull wire through back of basket; twist to secure. Cover foam with sheet moss; mist moss lightly with water.

3 Insert sprigs of eucalyptus into foam; fan out evenly.

4 Insert filler materials into arrangement, one variety at a time, spacing evenly.

GARDEN BOXES

In European design, individual elements are grouped in separate areas instead of being mixed throughout the arrangement. European-style floral arrangements resembling miniature gardens fit well into casual living environments; a more formal look can be achieved by using decorative containers of brass or painted ceramic.

Fruits and berries can be interspersed among flowers for visual contrast. Garden boxes can be made with materials of varying heights, placing taller materials in the center or back of the container and shorter materials along the edges. Or use materials of uniform height arranged in geometric patterns, as on page 80.

HOW TO MAKE A GARDEN BOX OF VARYING HEIGHTS

MATERIALS

- Dried larkspur and limonium or other line materials.
- Dried strawflowers, globe amaranth, and lavender or other secondary flowers.
- Preserved leatherleaf or other dried foliage.
- Artificial fruits, such as apples and grapes, on wire or wooden stems.

- Rectangular container.
- Floral foam for dried arranging.
- Sheet moss.
- Wire cutter; serrated knife; scissors.
- Floral pins.

1 Insert floral foam into container, and cover with moss; secure with floral pins (page 23). Trim off excess moss with scissors, or tuck excess into sides of container.

2 Fill about one-third of container on left side with larkspur or tallest line material, staying 1½" (3.8 cm) away from edges. Insert limonium about 2" (5 cm) away from larkspur.

3 Insert wired apples (page 24) between the two line materials, near base. Place grape clusters in front of the larkspur, inserting one slightly higher than the other; allow them to cascade downward.

4 Insert the remaining flowers around line materials, clustering the flowers by variety. Place longer stems near the center and the shorter stems near the outer edges. Stems closest to the center point upward, and stems closer to the outer edges point outward.

5 Insert leatherleaf to fill in any bare areas; intersperse among flowers, if necessary.

HOW TO MAKE A GARDEN BOX OF UNIFORM HEIGHT

MATERIALS

- Dried materials such as miniature artichokes, nigella pods, cockscomb, pomegranates, poppy pods, strawflowers, and garlic bulbs.
- Rectangular container.
- Floral foam for dried arranging.

- Sheet moss.
- Wire cutter; serrated knife.
- String.
- Hot glue gun and glue sticks.

1 Insert foam into container, and cover (page 23). For dried materials with stems, cut the stems 1" to 1½" (2.5 to 3.8 cm) below flower head or pod.

2 Divide container into sections of equal size, using string. Apply hot glue to stems or underside of dried materials; insert a different variety into each section, keeping height of floral materials even.

Thatched box *(left) combines lavender, roses, and rye in a parallel design, with equal space devoted to each. Floral materials rise 10" (25 cm) above the rim of the container.*

Shadow box *is filled with colorful flower heads, arranged in diagonal rows. The flowers are glued to a moss-covered sheet of foam board cut to fit in the shadow box.*

Wooden box *(right) contains grains, cattails, sunflowers, and poppy pods, arranged in vertical groupings. An array of dried and artificial fruits is inserted near the base.*

GARDEN BASKETS

Floor baskets containing potted florals bring a garden look into any interior. Use one as an accent near a fireplace or next to a favorite chair. This versatile basket arrangement also works well in a bedroom or entryway. It is made by placing three clay pots into a large basket, filling them with dried naturals, and surrounding them with moss.

HOW TO MAKE A GARDEN BASKET

MATERIALS

• Dried roses, larkspur, and oregano or other dried materials.

• Basket with handle, about 15" × 18" (38 × 46 cm).

• Three clay pots, about 6" (15 cm) in diameter.

• Floral foam for dried arranging.

• Spanish moss and sheet moss.

• Wire cutter; serrated knife.

• Hot glue gun and glue sticks.

1 Cut thin layer of foam to fit inside bottom of basket. Secure foam to basket, using hot glue. Cover bottoms of pots with hot glue, and press them into foam base, allowing pots to tip outward slightly, if desired.

2 Cut foam into pieces, and wedge into the area between pots and basket, keeping height of foam 2" (5 cm) below top edges of pots. Cover foam with sheet moss, securing it with hot glue. Also insert foam into clay pots, and cover with Spanish moss (page 23).

3 Insert one variety of dried natural into each pot, starting at center of pot and working out in a circle until the desired fullness is achieved. Stems in outer rows may be shorter than stems in center. Within a single variety, flowers may be positioned on each side of the handle. Fill in around edges of pots with additional Spanish moss, if desired.

SALAL & BOXWOOD WREATHS

Wreaths beautifully accent doors and walls, whether decorated for a particular season or embellished to coordinate with the decorating scheme of a room. Long-lasting beauty can be achieved by using everlasting foliage for the base and dried or preserved flowers for embellishments. Fresh salal or boxwood is an ideal choice for the base. About a week after the wreath is made, the leaves dry and curl, resulting in a beautiful display of medium to pale green foliage. To preserve the wreath's beauty, hang it away from humidity and direct sunlight. The foliage can be secured to either a wire or straw base, in small bunches or one stem at a time, depending on the fullness of the stems.

HOW TO MAKE A WIRE-BASE SALAL WREATH

MATERIALS

- Fresh salal.
- Dried roses or other dominant flowers.
- Preserved statice or other filler flowers.
- Wire wreath base.

- 22-gauge or 24-gauge paddle floral wire, cut in lengths of 15" to 18" (38 to 46 cm).
- Wire cutter.
- Hot glue gun and glue sticks.

1 Cut fresh salal into lengths ranging from 6" to 8" (15 to 20.5 cm). Cluster four to six lengths together, and wrap with wire. Place cluster on the wire base; secure by wrapping wire from cluster around the base, crossing it in back, and twisting ends together in front.

2 Secure additional salal clusters to base, overlapping each to conceal wire, until entire base is covered.

3 Secure embellishments to wreath, using hot glue. Insert dominant flowers first, followed by filler flowers; space all embellishments evenly throughout wreath.

4 Hang wreath in desired location, and allow to dry. Rotate wreath occasionally while drying, so the leaves curl evenly around the wreath's natural curve.

HOW TO MAKE A STRAW-BASE SALAL WREATH

MATERIALS

- Ready-made straw wreath.
- Fresh salal; fresh seeded eucalyptus.
- Dried roses and cockscomb or other dried flowers.
- Dried bear grass.

- Sheet moss.
- Wire cutter; floral pins; floral tape.
- 3" (7.5 cm) floral picks with wire.
- Hot glue gun and glue sticks.

1 Secure sheet moss to the top and sides of straw wreath, using hot glue. Mist the sheet moss lightly before securing, if desired, to make it more pliable.

2 Cut fresh salal stems to within 2" to 3" (5 to 7.5 cm) of lower leaves, using wire cutter; secure several stems to wreath, using floral pins. Stagger salal, covering inside, top, and outside of wreath.

3 Continue covering wreath with salal, overlapping as necessary to conceal floral pins. It is not necessary to cover moss entirely, since it contributes to the design.

4 Cut dried flower stems to lengths ranging from 4" to 6" (10 to 15 cm); wire them to floral picks as on page 24. Insert dried flowers into wreath as desired.

5 Insert seeded eucalyptus into wreath, securing with hot glue. Conceal ends of eucalyptus under salal, and weave branches through salal to hold them in place. Wire several stems of bear grass to floral picks, and insert into wreath as desired.

6 Hang wreath in desired location, and allow to dry. Rotate wreath occasionally while drying, so the leaves curl evenly around the wreath's natural curve.

HOW TO MAKE A WIRE-BASE OR STRAW-BASE BOXWOOD WREATH

1 Make wire-base wreath as on page 86, steps 1 and 2, or make straw-base wreath, opposite, steps 1 to 3; substitute fresh boxwood for salal. Attach embellishments such as pomegranates, roses, artichokes, pepper grass, and pepper berries to wreath, securing them with hot glue.

2 Hang wreath in desired location, and allow to dry. Rotate the wreath occasionally while drying, so leaves curl evenly around the wreath's natural curve.

Grapevine wreaths can complement any decorating style. Available at craft stores, grapevine bases come in a variety of sizes. Adding honeysuckle vine to the base can enlarge the size and create a loose, airy design with a woodsy look. A compact design can be made by covering parts of a grapevine wreath with sheet moss, creating a solid base for securing flower heads. Embellish the wreath with a wine bottle, clusters of grapes, and clay pots for the wine-country wreath shown here. Or choose from a variety of other embellishments to make the wreaths on pages 92 and 93.

MATERIALS

- Grapevine wreath.
- Honeysuckle vine.
- Dried hydrangeas and lavender.
- Mixed dried herbs.
- Silk ivy.
- Artificial grape clusters.
- Two clay pots.
- Empty wine bottle.
- Raffia.
- Wire cutter; 22-gauge paddle floral wire.
- Hot glue gun and glue sticks.

GRAPEVINE WREATHS

HOW TO MAKE A WINE-COUNTRY GRAPEVINE WREATH

1 Attach several strands of honeysuckle vine to wreath, securing with floral wire. Wrap vine loosely around wreath, allowing the strands to extend from the grapevine base; secure.

2 Apply hot glue to bottom of a wine bottle, and insert it into clay pot. Wrap floral wire below rim of pot, twisting to secure it; leave 5" (12.5 cm) ends. Glue wire to pot on two sides. Secure pot to wreath, using wire ends; glue pot to the wreath.

3 Tie raffia around pot to conceal wire and glue. Glue pieces of moss to wreath as desired.

4 Break remaining clay pot. Glue large pieces near base of pot with wine bottle; glue smaller pieces to wreath as desired.

5 Cut ivy apart; insert stems into wreath, securing with hot glue. Weave ivy around honeysuckle vines.

6 Insert grape clusters into wreath, securing with hot glue; concentrate clusters near wine bottle.

7 Apply hot glue to hydrangeas; secure to wreath. Bundle lavender, and place at bottom. Fill in bare areas with dried herbs; secure.

Heart wreath is embellished with sheet moss, potted roses, lavender bunches, and pepper berries.

Miniature wreaths are paired for impact. Sheet moss, pansies, and yellow rosebuds accent the wreaths for a romantic look.

Fruit wreath (opposite), wrapped with silver-dollar eucalyptus and artificial maple leaves, is covered with artificial fruit and dried fruit slices. Pinecones and sticks give the arrangement a woodsy look.

Autumn wreath has a grapevine base with added foliage. Fruits, vegetables, hydrangeas, poppy pods, and potted sunflowers embellish the wreath. Honeysuckle vine encircles the wreath.

A grapevine swag is easily made from a purchased grapevine wreath that has been cut in half. Hang a swag above a fireplace, or use it to decorate a wall.

Embellish the swag as desired to coordinate it with the surrounding decorating scheme. Flowers such as larkspur may replace the caspia, and a rose bundle may be substituted for the wheat sheaf.

MATERIALS

- Purchased grapevine wreath.
- Eucalyptus in two colors or other line materials.
- Dried canella berries or other desired berries.
- Dried caspia or other filler material.
- Dried wheat sheaf or other bundled material.
- 22-gauge or 24-gauge paddle floral wire; wire cutter.
- Hot glue gun and glue sticks.

HOW TO MAKE A GRAPEVINE SWAG

1 Cut the grapevine wreath in half, using a wire cutter or pruning shears. Join the halves as shown, securing them with wire.

2 Apply hot glue liberally to ends of eucalyptus, working with one color at a time; insert pieces around center of swag, spacing evenly and varying placement depth.

3 Apply glue to stems of canella berries, and insert into swag; intersperse berries among eucalyptus, varying placement depth.

4 Attach wheat sheaf to center of arrangement, applying glue generously to the sheaf and pressing it firmly into place. Hold for 5 minutes, to allow time for glue to set.

5 Apply glue to sprigs of caspia; insert into garland to fill in any bare areas as necessary.

HUCKLEBERRY
SWAGS

Swags of huckleberry can embellish any room in your home. These swags may be either arched or divided, offering two different looks. Make your own base of twigs for the arched swag shown here. Or use a purchased base for the divided swag on page 98. Embellish arched and divided swags with silk or dried flowers, or a combination of both.

Similar looks can be achieved by substituting birch, curly willow, or blueberry branches for the huckleberry. Branches of many varieties may be purchased from floral shops, or you may gather your own. Purchased swag bases are often available in birch and other branches.

HOW TO MAKE AN ARCHED HUCKLEBERRY SWAG

MATERIALS

- Huckleberry branches or other desired branches.
- Maidenhair fern and fresh heather or other fillers.
- Silk peonies or other dominant flowers.
- Dried sarracenia and silk roses or other secondary flowers.

- Grape clusters or other artificial fruit.
- Dried bear grass.
- Wire wreath base with attached wire fasteners.
- Wire cutter; floral tape.
- Hot glue gun and glue sticks.

1 Cut the wire wreath base apart, and spread it to form an arch. Secure bunches of huckleberry to the base, wrapping the wreath fasteners around bunches.

2 Cut fern into sprigs, ranging from 8" to 10" (20.5 to 25.5 cm); insert into swag at various angles, securing with hot glue. Insert heather into the swag, securing it with hot glue.

3 Cut the flower stems to lengths ranging from 6" to 10" (15 to 25.5 cm). Insert peonies, then roses, spacing them evenly throughout swag; secure with hot glue.

4 Insert grape clusters into the swag, securing them with hot glue. Insert sarracenia, spacing it evenly; secure with hot glue.

5 Make six to eight bunches of bear grass by securing ends of several stems together with floral tape. Apply glue to ends of bunches; insert, spacing them evenly to soften arrangement.

HOW TO MAKE A DIVIDED HUCKLEBERRY SWAG

MATERIALS

- Purchased divided swag base from huckleberry or other branches.
- Silk begonia or other leafy silk plant.
- Three silk delphiniums or other linear silk flowers.
- Dried rushes and leptosporum or other dried filler flowers.
- Artificial berries or other fruit.
- Wire cutter; hot glue gun and glue sticks.

1 Insert one stem of delphinium into each side of swag; secure with hot glue. Cut remaining stem of delphinium into pieces; set aside.

2 Cut rushes and leptosporum into lengths ranging from 5" to 8" (12.5 to 20.5 cm); glue some rushes to each side of swag, following the direction of the huckleberry branches and spacing evenly.

3 Cut stems from begonia plant, using wire cutter. Add floral picks, if necessary (page 24). Apply glue to the ends; insert stems evenly into the swag.

4 Insert some of the leptosporum into each side of swag; secure with glue. Fill in any bare areas with delphinium pieces. Glue the berries close to center.

FLORAL BUNDLES

Flowers may be bundled together to create a floral accent with a variety of uses. A floral bundle may be hung on a door or bedpost, or be placed on a tabletop. Floral bundles may be made from herbs to decorate the kitchen, from flowers to decorate a bedroom, or from evergreen branches to decorate the foyer for the holidays.

HOW TO MAKE FLORAL BUNDLES

MATERIALS

- Silk roses or other dominant flowers.
- Silk lilacs in two colors or other secondary flowers.
- Silk gingko or other foliage.
- Rubber band.
- Ribbon or raffia for bow.

1 Lay the foliage on a flat surface, fanning stems as shown, to create a base.

2 Place lilacs on top of foliage, in a fan shape. Insert the smallest roses; tuck them under the lilacs, next to foliage. Place largest roses on top of lilacs. Extend length of floral stems, if necessary (page 24).

3 Secure ends of stems together, using a rubber band. Cover the rubber band with raffia or ribbon. Trim ends of stems even, if desired.

FLEXIBLE GARLANDS

Garlands are versatile accessories for any room. They can be draped over headboards, shelves, pictures, or doorways. Flexible silk garlands are easily made by twisting wired flowers to an ivy garland. Nonwired materials can be attached to the garland, if desired, by securing them with floral wire.

HOW TO MAKE A FLEXIBLE GARLAND

MATERIALS

- Silk roses or other dominant flowers.
- Silk alstroemeria and astilbe or other secondary flowers.
- Silk miniature roses or other filler flowers.
- One 9-ft. (2.75 m) silk ivy garland.
- Two silk ivy plants, one solid green and one variegated.
- 22-gauge paddle floral wire and wire cutter, if silk flowers are not wired.

1 Cut stems from ivy plants; to add fullness, wrap the stems around garland, allowing some tendrils to extend.

2 Insert roses, spacing them evenly throughout the garland; secure by wrapping the stems around garland.

3 Insert astilbe into garland between roses, wrapping the stems around garland. Insert alstroemeria, spacing evenly; wrap the stems around garland.

4 Insert miniature roses to fill in any bare areas; wrap stems around garland.

SHAPED GARLANDS

Delicate-looking floral garlands add a romantic touch to walls or tables. For impact, drape a garland over a large mirror or shape one around a doorway to soften the straight lines and square corners. A shaped garland can also serve as a centerpiece when arranged down the center of a dining room table.

Create the base of the garland by encasing an evergreen garland in Spanish moss. For longer garlands, secure two or more evergreen garlands together.

MATERIALS

- One 6-ft. (1.85 m) evergreen garland.
- Silk hydrangeas and wild roses or other dominant flowers.
- Silk freesia or other secondary flowers.
- Silk baby's breath, astilbe, and wild berry sprays or other filler materials.
- Two 9-ft. (2.75 m) ivy garlands.
- Silk ivy plant.
- Berry vine.
- Spanish moss.
- Huckleberry twigs and honeysuckle vine, optional.
- Ribbon, optional.
- Fishing line.
- Wire cutter.
- Hot glue gun and glue sticks.

HOW TO MAKE A SHAPED GARLAND

1 Surround evergreen garland with Spanish moss, so the evergreen is barely visible; moss adheres to garland. Tie fishing line to garland at one end, and spiral it around the garland, encasing the moss; tie fishing line at opposite end. (White cord was used for clarity.)

2 Wrap ivy garlands around base in opposite directions, twisting vines around base to secure. Wrap berry vine around evergreen garland, allowing some tendrils to extend. Cut stems from ivy plant, and glue stems to garland, allowing some tendrils to extend.

3 Cut all flower stems to lengths ranging from 3" to 5" (7.5 to 12.5 cm). Secure hydrangeas and wild roses, one variety at a time, by applying hot glue to lower 1½" (3.8 cm) of stems.

4 Secure freesia to garland, as in step 3. Space the flowers evenly throughout the garland.

5 Apply glue to ends of the filler flowers, and insert them into the garland, one variety at a time, to fill in any bare areas. Insert twigs, vines, and ribbon, if desired.

HONEYSUCKLE GARLANDS

A decorative honeysuckle garland can adorn a table, wall, or mantel. Garlands can be filled with wisps of greenery or short, dense foliage, depending on the lengths of the floral materials used.

Garlands made of dried materials are fragile, and large garlands can be difficult to carry and arrange after they are finished. Therefore, you may want to construct the garland in the location where it will be displayed.

HOW TO MAKE A HONEYSUCKLE GARLAND

MATERIALS

- Honeysuckle vines.
- Preserved plumosa or other foliage.
- Silk and parchment roses or other dominant flowers.
- Dried pepper berries and nigella pods or other secondary materials.

- Dried pepper grass, statice, and veronica or other filler materials.
- Wire cutter.
- Paddle floral wire.
- Ribbon.

1 Cut the honeysuckle vines to arcs of desired lengths; secure together, using floral wire.

2 Insert sprigs of plumosa into vines until the desired fullness is achieved; secure with hot glue. Short stems make a more compact design.

3 Insert largest rose into center of garland to create a focal point. Insert remaining roses, spacing them evenly throughout garland; secure with hot glue.

4 Insert pepper berries so they radiate from central focal point; space evenly. Insert nigella pods, spacing evenly throughout.

5 Insert pepper grass, statice, and veronica, one variety at a time, radiating from the focal point. Insert ribbon into garland, forming loops at center; secure with hot glue.

TOPIARIES

Topiaries are unique floral arrangements that can be used alone or in pairs for a classic look on a fireplace mantel or buffet table. The base of a topiary can be a candlestick, as shown here. Or it can be a branch or a wooden dowel set into plaster of Paris. At the top, a cone or ball is covered with moss, vines, and other floral embellishments. The cone or ball may be either a Styrofoam® or grapevine form.

Candlestick topiaries are embellished with silk and dried floral materials for a romantic look.

Moss topiaries *are displayed as a pair. The topiary on the left has two twigs intertwined to form the trunk. The topiary on the right is a simple variation, with the moss-covered sphere glued directly to the rim of the pot.*

Floor topiary *is embellished with honeysuckle vine, dried greens, and dried floral materials.*

Fruit topiary *is decorated with fruit slices, artificial fruit, and ribbon.*

WREATHS, SWAGS & MORE

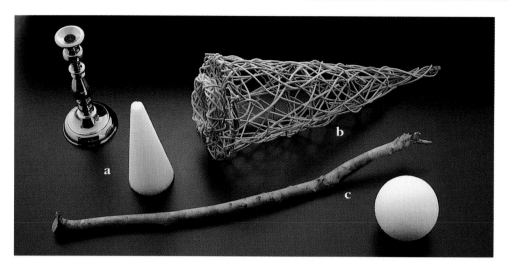

Topiaries can be made from a candlestick and a Styrofoam® cone **(a).** Or for a topiary set in plaster of Paris, you can use a branch and a grapevine cone **(b)** or Styrofoam ball **(c).**

HOW TO MAKE A TOPIARY WITH A CANDLESTICK BASE

MATERIALS

- Silk roses, hydrangeas, and wild roses or other dominant flowers.
- Silk rose hips and astilbe and dried lepidium or other filler flowers.
- Artificial berries; huckleberry or other twigs.

- Silk ivy or other leafy plant.
- Candlestick; Styrofoam cone.
- Spanish moss.
- Wire cutter; floral adhesive clay; floral pins.
- Hot glue gun and glue sticks.

1 Place a ring of floral adhesive clay around the outer rim of candlestick. Apply hot glue generously over top of candlestick; allow glue to cool slightly. Center the base of Styrofoam cone over the candlestick. Press cone down into glue and floral adhesive clay, twisting slightly to secure.

2 Cover the cone lightly with Spanish moss; secure with floral pins. Cut ivy stems from plant, using a wire cutter. Insert stems into foam; wrap ivy tightly around the cone, securing with floral pins. Insert the stems of berries into cone, spacing them evenly.

3 Cut rose stems to lengths of 2" (5 cm); insert into cone, one variety at a time, spacing them evenly. Insert the hydrangeas throughout topiary, spacing evenly. Extend the length of hydrangea stems, if necessary (page 24).

4 Cut lepidium, rose hips, and astilbe to lengths ranging from 3" to 6" (7.5 to 15 cm); insert evenly throughout topiary, one variety at a time. Bend stems, and shape flowers and leaves as necessary to balance arrangement and to cover any bare areas. Embellish with twigs.

HOW TO MAKE A TOPIARY WITH A PLASTER OF PARIS BASE

MATERIALS

- Floral materials, such as moss, artificial fruits, and dried naturals.
- Wooden box, ceramic pot, or other desired container.
- Grapevine or Styrofoam® cone or ball.
- Branch, twigs, or dowel for trunk.

- Plaster of Paris; disposable container for mixing.
- Heavy-duty aluminum foil.
- Saw, floral wire, and wire cutter may be needed for some projects, depending on floral materials selected.
- Hot glue gun and glue sticks.

1 Grapevine form. Line container with two layers of aluminum foil. Crumple foil loosely to shape of container, to allow room for plaster to expand as it dries; edge of foil should be about ¾" (2 cm) below top of container.

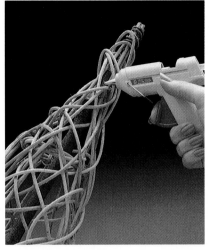

2 Insert trunk of tree into grapevine form as far as it will go. Place trunk in container, and adjust height of the topiary by cutting trunk to desired length. Secure grapevine form to trunk, using hot glue.

3 Mix the plaster of Paris, following manufacturer's instructions. Pour plaster into the container, filling to edge of foil. When plaster has started to thicken, insert trunk, making sure it stands straight. Support trunk, using tape as shown, until plaster has set.

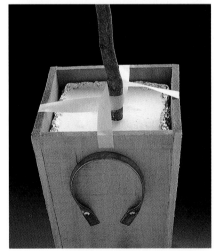

4 Conceal plaster with moss or items that will be used to decorate topiary. Embellish grapevine form as desired.

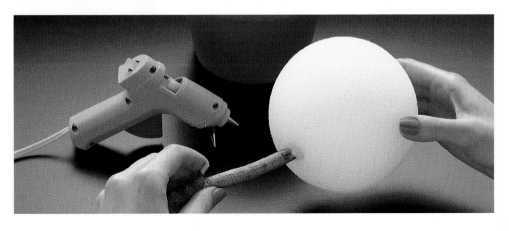

Styrofoam form. Prepare container as in step 1, above. Insert trunk of topiary into foam ball or cone to one-half the diameter of ball. Place trunk in the container, and adjust the height of topiary by cutting trunk to desired length. Apply hot glue into hole in foam ball; place ball on trunk. Continue as in steps 3 and 4, above.

Floral Accessories

A basket, box, or vase can be decorated with moss, leaves, or other floral materials to create a unique container for an arrangement. The base for the container may be made from a cardboard or wooden box, a glass vase, or a terra-cotta pot. The decorative containers may be embellished with a raffia or ribbon bow.

MATERIALS

- Basket, box, vase, or terra-cotta pot.
- Silk or preserved leaves, moss, pinecones, or flowers.
- Hot glue gun and glue sticks, or thick white craft glue.
- Raffia or ribbon, optional.

HOW TO MAKE DECORATIVE CONTAINERS

Leaves. Secure silk or preserved leaves in rows to vase or other container, using hot glue; overlap leaves as necessary to cover container. Leaves may be wrapped over the rim of the container, if desired. Embellish the container with raffia or ribbon as desired.

Pinecones. Cover cardboard box lightly with sheet moss; secure with hot glue. Cut the scales from one side of the pinecones, to make flat surface. Using hot glue, secure pinecones to sides of box with all pinecones facing in the same direction.

Moss. Secure sheet moss to sides of terra-cotta pot, using hot glue; cover the pot completely, and allow moss to extend slightly above the rim of the container.

Flowers. Secure flower petals to container, using thick white craft glue. For added embellishment, apply glue to the underside of flower heads and leaves; secure to the sides of the container.

DECORATING WIRE FORMS

Wire forms in various shapes and sizes can be covered with sheet moss for the look of a professionally groomed garden topiary. The forms, available from garden centers, craft stores, and mail-order suppliers, are first wrapped with wire mesh, then with the sheet moss, as shown below.

Other wire forms, such as bird cages, can be embellished with ivy vines, flowers, berries, and ribbons, using your creativity. Simply twist the vines around the wire forms, and use a hot glue gun to secure other embellishments.

HOW TO DECORATE WIRE FORMS

MATERIALS

- Wire form in desired shape, such as animal form.
- Wire mesh, such as chicken wire.
- Sheet moss.
- Wire cutter; paddle floral wire.

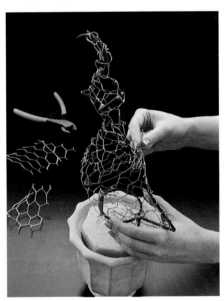

1 Place wire mesh over wire form, folding it around wire contours. Clip away any excess mesh, using a wire cutter; wrap wire ends around form as necessary to secure.

2 Mist the sheet moss lightly with water to make it more pliable. Cover wire form with sheet moss, securing it with floral wire.

Wire forms can be covered with sheet moss, as shown on the animal forms. Or accent wire forms like the bird cage and sphere topiary with vines, flowers, and foliage.

POMANDERS

Pomanders made from fragrant floral materials add a delicate aroma to a room. Hang pomanders decoratively in the center of a window or doorway. Or group them together to fill a bowl or basket, perhaps for a centerpiece on the dining-room table.

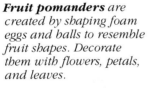

Fruit pomanders *are created by shaping foam eggs and balls to resemble fruit shapes. Decorate them with flowers, petals, and leaves.*

Pomander *is covered with rose petals. Rosebuds, plumosa, and ribbons, secured with hot glue, add a finishing touch to the top of the pomander. The pomander may be tied to a lamp pull or bedpost.*

Leaf-covered spheres *are decorated with leaves. The leaves may be secured with glue, or secure them with brads for a decorative accent. Combine spheres of different sizes and types, grouping them together in a basket.*

HOW TO MAKE FRUIT POMANDERS

MATERIALS

- Lavender, boxwood leaves, yarrow, rose petals, sunflower petals, globe amaranth, marigold petals or other desired floral materials.
- Dried or silk leaves, such as lemon verbena, pineapple, and grape.
- Twigs; cloves.
- Styrofoam® balls, eggs, and wreaths of various sizes, depending on the kinds and sizes of fruit desired.
- Wire cutter; serrated knife.
- Low-temperature glue gun and glue sticks; thick white craft glue.

1 Grapes. Apply white glue to small foam balls; roll the balls in lavender blossoms to cover. Allow to dry.

2 Form a grape cluster by securing several lavender-covered balls to 3" to 4" (7.5 to 10 cm) twig, using glue gun. Secure silk or dried leaf to end.

1 Pear. Press end of foam egg against table; roll gently from side to side to form shape for end of pear. Smooth the shape by pressing foam with fingers as necessary.

2 Apply white glue to foam; roll pear in boxwood leaves or yarrow to cover. Insert 2" (5 cm) twig into end of pear; secure, using glue gun.

1 Apple. Press a foam ball against table; roll lower two-thirds of ball gently from side to side to flatten and narrow slightly for bottom of apple.

2 Insert knife into top of apple at an angle; cut out a small cone shape about ½" (1.3 cm) long. Repeat at bottom of apple, cutting out a cone shape about ¼" (6 mm) long.

3 Smooth sharp edges by pressing foam with fingers. Apply white glue to foam, and roll in rose petals to cover. Insert 2" (5 cm) twig and lemon verbena leaves into top of apple; secure, using glue gun.

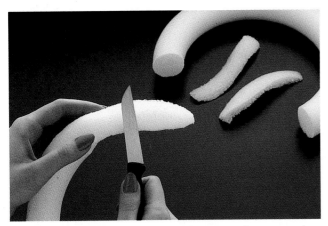

1 Banana. Cut 10" (25.5 cm) arc from Styrofoam wreath form; shape banana by trimming ends to points.

2 Apply white glue to foam; roll in sunflower petals to cover. Insert cloves into ends.

Pineapple. Trim lower end of foam egg to form flat base. Glue a stick into bottom of egg to make decorating easier. Apply glue to globe amaranth, using glue gun; insert pineapple leaves into top, securing with glue gun. Trim stick from base.

Orange. Make indentation in top and bottom of foam ball, using finger. Apply white glue to foam; roll in marigold petals to cover. Insert clove at each end.

HOW TO MAKE LEAF-COVERED POMANDERS

MATERIALS

- Styrofoam balls.
- Preserved, artificial, or fresh leaves.
- Low-temperature glue gun and glue sticks, or decorative brads.

Spheres with leaves. Secure leaves in rows to foam balls, using glue; each row overlaps leaves of previous row.

Spheres with leaves and brads. Secure leaves in rows to foam balls, inserting decorative brad at tip of each leaf to secure; each row overlaps leaves of previous row.

FLORAL ROOM ACCENTS

Chandelier is decorated with floral corsages made of silk and dried floral materials. The arms of the chandelier are wrapped with ivy and raffia.

Frame with a flat surface is embellished with silk roses, dried hydrangea, and poppy pods.

Basket (left) with moss-covered rim is embellished with dried peonies, hydrangeas, carnations, pepper berries, and salal leaves.

HOW TO ADD FLORAL ACCENTS TO A CHANDELIER

MATERIALS

- Floral materials as desired.
- Wire cutter; stem wire.

- Floral tape.
- Raffia or ribbon.

1 Add wire stems to individual floral materials, if necessary (page 24). Make raffia loops, and secure to wire stems. Combine materials into three small bunches; secure each bunch at top of stems, using floral tape.

2 Make floral corsage by securing the three floral bunches together 1" (2.5 cm) from top of stems, using floral tape.

3 Cut all but two stems from corsage. Bend and shape stems and leaves to achieve desired look. Secure the corsage to the chandelier, using the remaining stems.

HOW TO ADD FLORAL ACCENTS TO FRAMES & BASKETS

MATERIALS

- Floral materials as desired.
- Sheet moss.

- Frame or basket.
- Wire cutter; hot glue gun and glue sticks.

1 Frame. Cover frame with sheet moss, securing it with hot glue. Mist moss lightly, if desired, to make it more pliable.

2 Secure embellishments to frame as desired, using hot glue.

Basket. Cover the rim of the basket with sheet moss as in step 1. Secure embellishments to rim as desired, using hot glue.

Serving tray *is embellished with a ring of silk ivy and flowers. The ivy vine encircles the platter, and the ends are twisted together. Stems of silk flowers are wrapped around the vine to embellish it.*

Votive candle *sits inside a hollowed-out dried artichoke that is sprayed with gold metallic paint.*

Coordinating arrangement and napkin accent *(opposite) make this breakfast tray festive. For the napkin accent, secure silk blossoms together with floral tape. French ribbon, tied around the napkin, conceals the tape.*

Goblet, place card holder, and napkin *(right) are embellished with dried flowers. The flowers are bundled together with floral tape and wrapped with ribbon. An additional ribbon secures the floral bundle to the goblet and the napkin. Hot glue holds the bundle to the place card holder.*

INDEX

CREDITS

COWLES
Creative Publishing, Inc.

President: Iain Macfarlane
Executive V.P.: William B. Jones

DECORATING WITH SILK & DRIED
FLOWERS
Created by: The Editors of
  Cowles Creative Publishing

Books available in this series:
*Bedroom Decorating, Creative Window
Treatments, Decorating for Christmas,
Decorating the Living Room, Creative
Accessories for the Home, Decorating with
Silk & Dried Flowers, Kitchen & Bathroom
Ideas, Decorating the Kitchen, Decorative
Painting, Decorating Your Home for
Christmas, Decorating for Dining &
Entertaining, Decorating with Fabric &
Wallcovering, Decorating the Bathroom,
Decorating with Great Finds, Affordable
Decorating, Picture-Perfect Walls, More
Creative Window Treatments, Outdoor
Decor, The Gift of Christmas, Home
Accents in a Flash, Painted Illusions*

Executive Editor: Zoe A. Graul
Senior Technical Director: Rita C. Arndt
Technical Director: Dawn M. Anderson
Senior Project Manager: Joseph Cella
Project Manager: Diane Dreon-Krattiger
Senior Art Director: Lisa Rosenthal
Art Director: Stephanie Michaud
Writer: Dawn M. Anderson
Editor: Janice Cauley
Sample Supervisor: Carol Olson
Photo Coordinator: Diane Dreon-Krattiger
Senior Technical Photo Stylist: Bridget
  Haugh
Styling Director: Bobbette Destiche
Crafts Stylists: Coralie Sathre, Joanne
  Wawra
Artisans: Caren Carlson, Phyllis Galbraith,
  Linda Neubauer, Carol Pilot, Nancy
  Sundeen, Deborah Weber
*Vice President of Development Planning
  & Production:* Jim Bindas
Creative Photo Coordinator: Cathleen
  Shannon
Photo Studio Manager: Mike Parker
Assistant Studio Manager: Marcia
  Chambers
Lead Photographer: Bill Lindner
Photographers: Stuart Block, Rebecca
  Hawthorne, Mike Hehner, Rex Irmen,
  John Lauenstein, Mark Macemon, Paul
  Najlis, Charles Nields, Mike Parker,
  Robert Powers
Contributing Photographers: Kim
  Bailey, Kenton Cornett, Paul Markert,
  Brad Parker

Technical Photo Stylist: Susan Pasqual
Production Manager: Amelia Merz
Electronic Publishing Specialist: Joe Fahey
Production Staff: Adam Esco, Mike
  Hehner, Jeff Hickman, Janet Morgan,
  Robert Powers, Mike Schauer, Kay
  Wethern, Nik Wogstad
Shop Supervisor: Phil Juntti
Scenic Carpenters: John Nadeau, Mike
  Peterson, Greg Wallace
Consultants: Michael Basler, Nena
  Benhoff, Jill Englehart, Jackie Wilkinson
Contributors: C. M. Offray & Son, Inc.;
  Houseparts Inc.; Lion Ribbon Company;
  McCann Brothers; Sopp America, Inc.;
  Sullivan's; Watson Smith; Wildwood
  International

Printed on American paper by:
R. R. Donnelley & Sons Co.
00 99 98 97 / 5 4 3 2 1

Cowles Creative Publishing, Inc. offers
a variety of how-to books. For
information write:
  Cowles Creative Publishing
    Subscriber Books
  5900 Green Oak Drive
  Minnetonka, MN 55343